CONTENTS

Jórvík 4

Putting Jórvík on the map 6

Meet the people 8

Arrive by river 10

Where to stay 12

Feast like a king 14

Hit the shops 16

Dress like a Viking 18

Try being a blacksmith 20

Visit the cemetery 22

Learn some Old Norse 24

Make time for the holy Minster 26

Visit quick! 28

Glossary and Further Information 30

Index 32

JÓRVÍK

Welcome to Jórvík, known today as York. This English city was once conquered and controlled by the Vikings for over 70 years. In CE 866, the Vikings invaded the Northumbrian city and built it into a bustling commercial centre with a booming population. In the 21st century, archaeologists have dug 5 metres underneath the city of York to rediscover the Viking settlement. With time-travel technology, however, we can journey back to discover the city for ourselves. So, buckle up and brace yourself to meet the Vikings: the Scandinavian warriors with a fierce reputation.

Your time travel guide

Congratulations for buying this Time Travel Guidebook – the must-have companion for travellers journeying into the past. The guidebook will give you expert advice on where to stay, what to see and how best to spend your time in Jórvík. Top travel tips throughout will tell you what to bring, where to shop and which local customs to avoid.

TIME TRAVEL GUIDES

VIKING BRITAIN
and
Jórvík

Ben Hubbard

W
FRANKLIN W
LONDON•SYDN

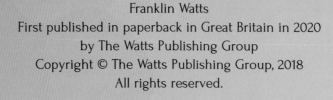

Franklin Watts
First published in paperback in Great Britain in 2020
by The Watts Publishing Group
Copyright © The Watts Publishing Group, 2018
All rights reserved.

Illustration and Design: Collaborate Agency
Editor: Sarah Silver

ISBN 978 1 4451 5733 7

Picture credits:
p.4-5: © jremes84 / Shutterstock.com.
Every attempt has been made to clear copyright. Should there be any inadvertent
oversight ... ...ply to the publisher for rectification.

Printed in Dubai

Franklin Watts
An imprint of
Hachette Children's Group
The Watts Publishing Group
Carmelite House
Victoria Embankment
London EC4Y 0DZ

An Hachette UK Company
www.hachette.co.uk
www.franklinwatts.co.uk

FSC
www.fsc.org

MIX
Paper from
responsible sources
FSC® C104740

Guesswork

Shown here in the 21st century, York is a city in the north of England where archaeologists have found many well-preserved objects and ruins that help them understand the lives of people who lived in Jórvík hundreds of years ago.

Look out for

Silver and slaves. Silver is the main currency in the 10th century. People are abducted as slaves from towns in Ireland, Britain and France and sold in markets as far away as Russia and Turkey.

Top Tip

What to pack

A toothbrush. The Vikings never brushed their teeth, which were often damaged on their rock-hard bread. So, make sure to chew carefully when you're there.

PUTTING JÓRVÍK ON THE MAP

The Romans built a fort called Eboracum on the site of modern-day York, which became a small but important Anglo-Saxon city called Eoforwic. After the Viking invasion, Scandinavians and Anglo-Saxons flocked to Eoforwic (which they renamed Jórvík) and its population rose from 2,000 to 10,000 people. This has made Jórvík a lively city with plenty of places to visit. Each of these places has been highlighted on this map. To learn more about them, simply turn to the page numbers given in the map key.

A strategic city

The Vikings like Jórvík for the same reason the Romans did: its position between two rivers makes it easy to defend as well as providing access to the city by boat. Jórvík is the main city in the region of England known as the Danelaw. The Danelaw is all the territory controlled by the Vikings in the 9th century. It is made up of 14 shires that include Lincoln, Essex, Cambridge, Norfolk, Middlesex and Buckingham.

- English Territory
- Danish or Norse Territory
- Celtic Territory
- Swamp or Alluvium

Jorvik

The Danelaw

Wales

Cambridge

London

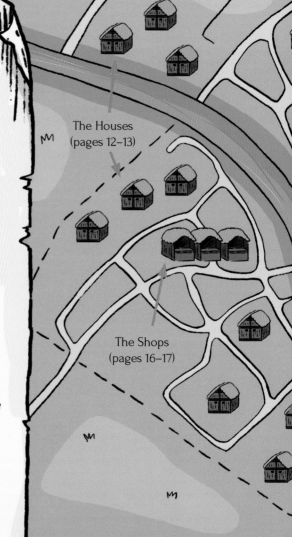

The Houses
(pages 12–13)

The Shops
(pages 16–17)

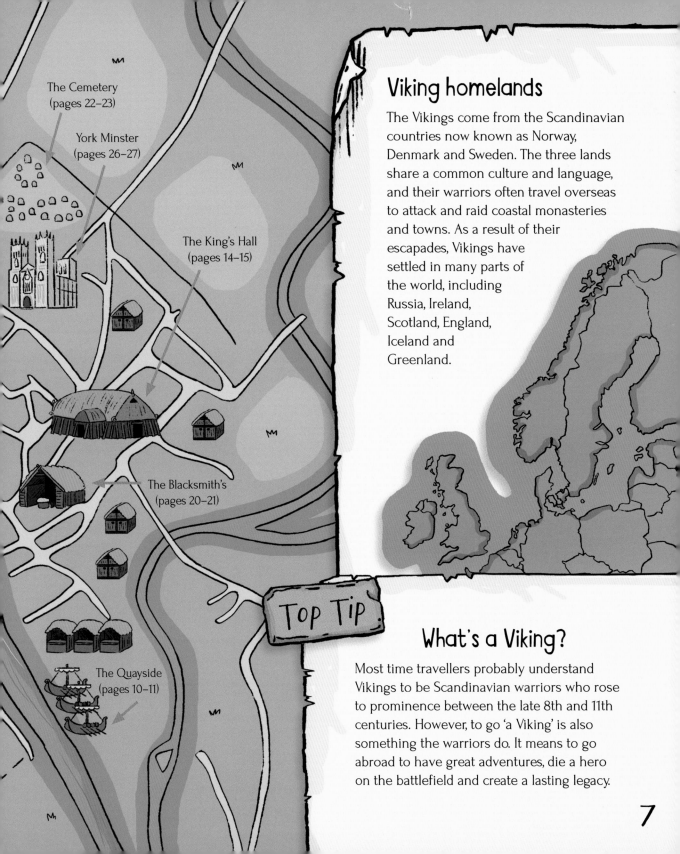

The Cemetery
(pages 22–23)

York Minster
(pages 26–27)

The King's Hall
(pages 14–15)

The Blacksmith's
(pages 20–21)

The Quayside
(pages 10–11)

Viking homelands

The Vikings come from the Scandinavian countries now known as Norway, Denmark and Sweden. The three lands share a common culture and language, and their warriors often travel overseas to attack and raid coastal monasteries and towns. As a result of their escapades, Vikings have settled in many parts of the world, including Russia, Ireland, Scotland, England, Iceland and Greenland.

Top Tip

What's a Viking?

Most time travellers probably understand Vikings to be Scandinavian warriors who rose to prominence between the late 8th and 11th centuries. However, to go 'a Viking' is also something the warriors do. It means to go abroad to have great adventures, die a hero on the battlefield and create a lasting legacy.

MEET THE PEOPLE

Time travellers may find it unnerving to meet real Viking warriors in the flesh. They have a well-earned bloodthirsty reputation. Tall, armed and often covered in tattoos, Vikings are brought up on tales of war and conquest. However, they can also be hospitable and they love a good story. So, smile, stay calm and don't challenge anyone to a duel!

The first raiders

You might hear Vikings boasting about their first famous English raid on the monastery at Lindisfarne, in CE 793. A longship full of Vikings attacked the monastery, slaughtered the monks, stole their silver and gold and sailed home. Similar hit-and-run raids took place for many decades in Britain, Ireland and France. But as time went on, whole Viking armies attacked bigger targets, such as Paris and London.

Settling in

After the Vikings invaded Jórvík, they settled down and built new homes there. The Vikings of Jórvík often lived as shopkeepers, merchants and craftspeople, and their goods were sold across the Viking trade networks.

The English invasion

Lucky time travellers may be taken to see the graves of those warriors who died during the Great Invasion of CE 866. Then, a 3,000-strong Viking army led by Ivar the Boneless captured Jórvík (then called Eoforwic) and went on to conquer the Anglo-Saxon kingdoms of Northumbria, Mercia and East Anglia. Wessex, ruled over by King Alfred, withstood the invasion. In 878, King Alfred signed a peace treaty agreeing the Vikings could rule over much of north and eastern England. This land became known as the Danelaw (see map page 6).

Top Tip

Watch out for...

Snake pits. Legends tell of how the Anglo-Saxons executed Viking warrior Ragnar Lodbrok by throwing him into one. Rumours have it that Ragnar's son, Ivar the Boneless, ordered the conquest of England to avenge his father's death.

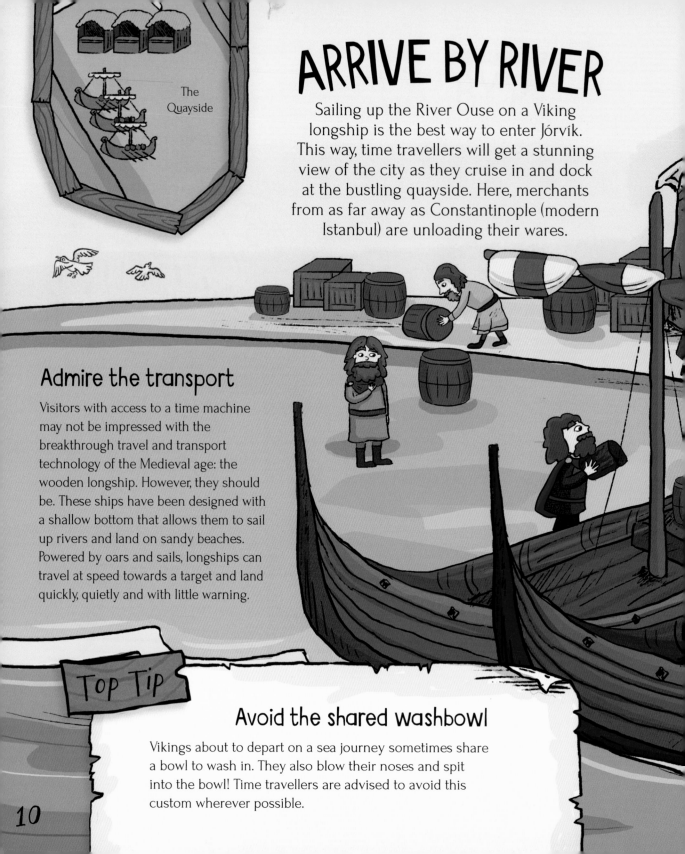

ARRIVE BY RIVER

Sailing up the River Ouse on a Viking longship is the best way to enter Jórvík. This way, time travellers will get a stunning view of the city as they cruise in and dock at the bustling quayside. Here, merchants from as far away as Constantinople (modern Istanbul) are unloading their wares.

The Quayside

Admire the transport

Visitors with access to a time machine may not be impressed with the breakthrough travel and transport technology of the Medieval age: the wooden longship. However, they should be. These ships have been designed with a shallow bottom that allows them to sail up rivers and land on sandy beaches. Powered by oars and sails, longships can travel at speed towards a target and land quickly, quietly and with little warning.

Top Tip

Avoid the shared washbowl

Vikings about to depart on a sea journey sometimes share a bowl to wash in. They also blow their noses and spit into the bowl! Time travellers are advised to avoid this custom wherever possible.

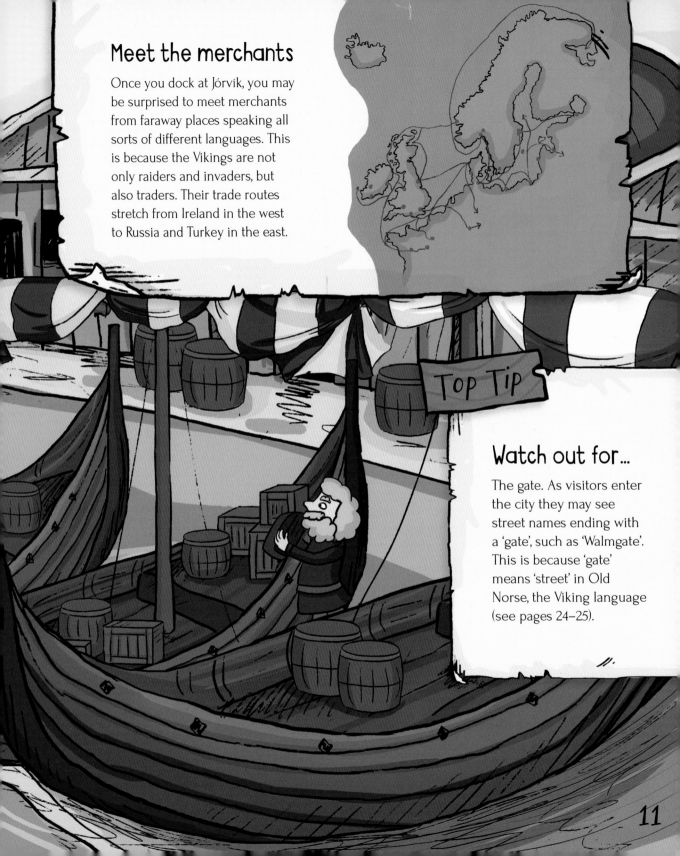

Meet the merchants

Once you dock at Jórvík, you may be surprised to meet merchants from faraway places speaking all sorts of different languages. This is because the Vikings are not only raiders and invaders, but also traders. Their trade routes stretch from Ireland in the west to Russia and Turkey in the east.

Top Tip

Watch out for...

The gate. As visitors enter the city they may see street names ending with a 'gate', such as 'Walmgate'. This is because 'gate' means 'street' in Old Norse, the Viking language (see pages 24–25).

11

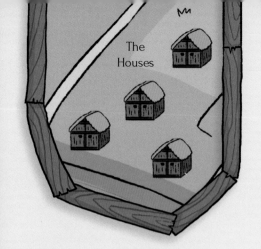

The Houses

WHERE TO STAY

Time travellers may be expecting to stay in a traditional Viking longhouse covered with grass turf. However, the houses in Jórvík are a mixture of Viking and Anglo-Saxon styles. The homes are made from wood with thatched roofs and an outside toilet in the backyard. However, do not expect any modern conveniences, such as running water.

Say goodbye to sanitation

Time travellers will quickly realise that the Vikings are not too fussed about personal hygiene. Their toilets are simply a hole in the ground and they don't wash their hands! As such, the people of Jórvík suffer from intestinal worms, which give them terrible stomach pains and even shorten their lives. So, time travellers should come prepared by packing some liquid handwash.

Top Tip

Bring your own toilet paper

In Jórvík, toilet paper usually consists of old pieces of fabric and moss. Travellers from the 21st century may therefore want to bring their own.

A hearthy home

Your time in a Jórvík home will be spent around the hearth. It is the only source of heat in the house, so it burns constantly. Food stored in large casks is cooked over the hearth in iron pots and then eaten using spoons made of wood and bone. Vikings are great meat-eaters and cattle, sheep, pigs and chickens are eaten, as are fish from the rivers. Other favourite foodstuffs include wheat, barley, oats and fruit.

TOP TIP

After-dinner fun

Vital tasks such as spinning, weaving and wood-carving are often carried out after dinner, but Vikings are always up for some evening fun. They'll be keen to teach you Hnefatafl, a type of chess played on a chequered board with pieces made from antler, amber or wood.

13

The King's Hall

FEAST LIKE A KING

For an agreed amount of silver, visitors can visit the King's Hall in the old Roman gatehouse. Here, you'll be invited to experience one of the great events of the Jórvík calendar: a Viking feast. These can sometimes last for several days in a row, so get ready to party!

Let the feasting commence

A feast is often held to do business with other Vikings, or celebrate a victory or homecoming. When you enter the hall, you will see tapestries and torches on the walls, benches and tables laid out with the finest Viking tableware, and a roaring fire in the hearth. Food will be served around the clock until the feast ends, which will be several hours or days later. Alongside the food, lots of alcoholic drinks will be consumed. These include beer, fruit wines and mead, a drink made from honey. Beer is drunk from horns that need to be finished in one go, so the contents don't spill. It is also considered an insult to try and put down a half-drunk horn, so be careful!

Top Tip

Look out for ...

Fish and meat pickled in salt or whey. Whey is the watery part of milk that can preserve raw meats for long lengths of time. This is one way the Vikings store their meat over the cold winter months.

All about entertainment

To take some time out from all the eating and drinking, time travellers can sit and enjoy the live entertainment. This includes musicians playing lutes, flutes and pipes, as well as jugglers and acrobats and poetry-performing skalds. Skalds are an essential part of Viking hall life. They recite epic poems about their king's accomplishments as well as current and historical events. Their poems are full of colourful descriptions and heroic acts, and are very popular!

15

The Shops

HIT THE SHOPS

Coppergate is the name of the main shopping street in Jórvík. It is the perfect place to make a holiday purchase. Here, a row of front-facing shops and workshops sell a variety of goods made in England and abroad. Time-travelling shoppers will be spoilt for choice. The only question is: how much silver did you bring to spend?

Buy some local handicrafts

It may be interesting for time travellers to note the number of intricate items being created on Coppergate. Far from being mindless barbarians, the Vikings are expert craftspeople, capable of producing many beautiful objects. These include wooden bowls, cups and spoons; leather boots, scabbards and belts; and ornate silver jewellery, such as brooches, pins, rings and pendants.

Top Tip

Get it quick!

Some of the goods currently in hot demand in Jórvík are bone ice skates, antler combs and blue glass beads. If you see any of these, grab them while you can!

Find exotic foreign objects

Many exotic goods from abroad are brought in to Jórvík across the vast Viking trade networks. These include silks, shells and spices from the east and amber, walrus ivory and furs from the Scandinavian homelands. Painted pottery and quern stones to grind flour come from Germany, and gold and silver dress-pins are made in Ireland.

Top Tip

Insist on scales

Trustworthy Jórvík shopkeepers and merchants are always happy to weigh precious items made of silver or gold using scales. Some even have portable bronze scales that can be folded up and taken away. Make sure you insist on items being weighed before you buy them!

DRESS LIKE A VIKING

Both Viking men and women take a great deal of time over their appearance. As well as wearing the latest clothing styles, Vikings keep their hair and beards neatly clipped and use tweezers to remove stray hairs. Time travellers wanting to join in with Viking trends will have to wear black eye makeup – a fashion worn by both women and men.

Dress like a Viking man

To dress like a Viking man, time travellers should wear linen trousers and armbands, an undershirt and a large cloak that leaves the sword-arm free. Headbands are optional, but hair is worn long on the top and shaved at the sides and back.

Body art

Tattoos on the head, neck and body are encouraged. Time travellers should get their parents' permission to tattoo themselves, however.

Watch the threads

According to Viking law, it is a crime for a man to intentionally dirty or tear another man's clothes. The punishment is being outlawed. So, time travellers should watch where they step with all those long cloaks around!

Dress like a Viking woman

To dress like a Viking woman, time travellers will need to wear a long dress made of linen or wool that reaches down to their feet. Dresses are held in place by shoulder straps and large brooches and usually worn over a petticoat. Most Viking women also wear a brooch with keys or other useful implements hanging from it. To fit in you could also put on a warm cloak and leather shoes.

A wearable bank

When travelling abroad with their husbands, very wealthy Viking women wear a large amount of silver jewellery. This works like a type of portable bank, as the silver can be taken off and used to purchase things if needed.

19

The Blacksmith's

TRY BEING A BLACKSMITH

A blacksmith is of great importance to any Viking settlement and Jórvík is no different. This is because the blacksmith is responsible for one of the most important aspects of a Viking warrior's life – his weapons. The Jórvík blacksmith is currently offering time travellers the chance to make their own battle axe. Get in quick to take advantage of this generous offer.

Viking weaponry

A Viking's weapons are his prized possessions and buried with him after death for use in the afterlife. Time travellers will be invited to forge a battle axe with a bearded edge, a common weapon that every Viking can afford to buy. Swords are more costly and time consuming to make and only the richest and most powerful Vikings have one. The great swords carried by famous warriors are talked about by the skalds (see page 15) and given names such as 'Leg Biter', 'Life Taker' and 'Truce Breaker'.

Make some peaceful objects

Time travellers not into weaponry can make a range of other iron items used by the Vikings. These include horse spurs, candle holders, knives, hammers and chisels. Why not craft yourself a Viking-age belt buckle? Just ask the blacksmith how.

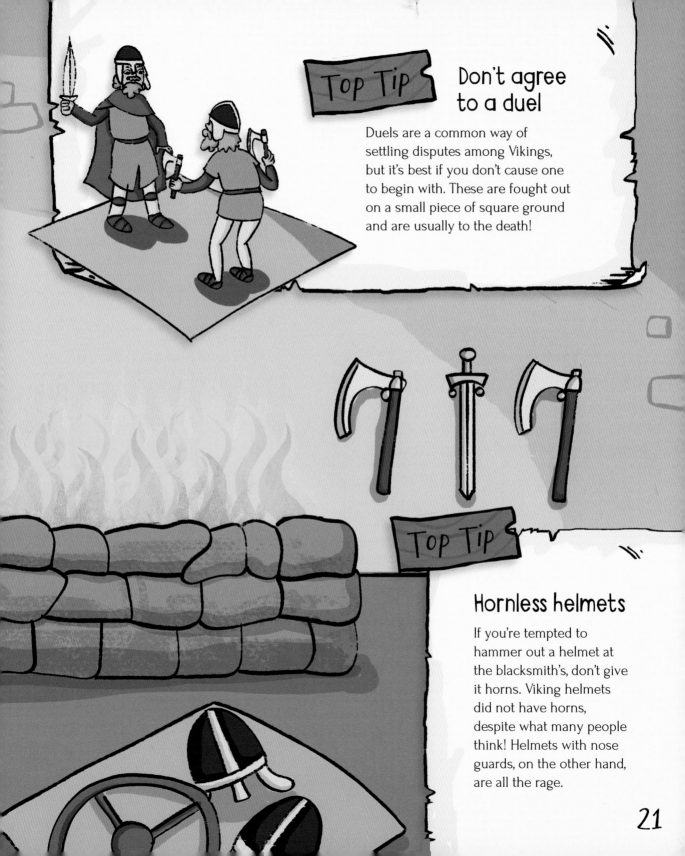

Don't agree to a duel

Duels are a common way of settling disputes among Vikings, but it's best if you don't cause one to begin with. These are fought out on a small piece of square ground and are usually to the death!

TOP TIP

Hornless helmets

If you're tempted to hammer out a helmet at the blacksmith's, don't give it horns. Viking helmets did not have horns, despite what many people think! Helmets with nose guards, on the other hand, are all the rage.

21

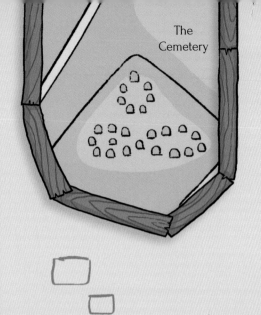

The Cemetery

VISIT THE CEMETERY

Although it sounds a little ghoulish, the main Jórvík cemetery is a must-see attraction for time-travelling tourists. It is here that the Vikings bury their dead under stone slabs. Burials are an extremely important part of Viking culture, as they mark the passing over of the dead to the afterlife beyond.

The final journey

As Jórvík residents will tell time travellers, a Viking warrior's death is a great occasion which begins his journey to Valhalla. Valhalla is the vast hall of the god Odin, where all honourable warriors go after their death. Here the warriors fill their time feasting and fighting and waiting for Ragnarök, the last great battle of the world. Female Vikings go to an afterlife field called Fólkvangr, which is ruled over by the goddess Freyja. Not all burials are the same: some Vikings are buried on board their longship, which is then set alight and pushed out to sea. Others are buried in massive burial mounds. Vikings who have converted to Christianity may be buried in a coffin or covered in cloth.

See the stones

Time travellers should take note that graves in Jórvík are marked with stones decorated with mythical creatures. Vikings also sometimes leave runestones (see pages 24–25). These runestones act as Viking memorials to their dead and the runes are carved onto the stone with a hammer and chisel. The runes say things like 'Hákon raised this monument in memory of Gunnarr, his son. He died in the west.' Images of serpents and dragons often accompany the burial inscriptions.

Top Tip

Objects for later?

The Vikings believe their favourite objects need to be buried with them for use in the afterlife. A Viking's weapons are therefore extremely important. What would you choose to take with you?

23

LEARN SOME OLD NORSE

In Jórvík, time travellers will hear many different languages. These may include Old English, Old Norse, Old Irish, Old Welsh and Old Frisian. Also known as the 'Danish tongue', Old Norse is the Viking language spoken exclusively by the people of Denmark, Norway and Sweden. Learning some Old Norse will help you get around – it may also be easier than you think!

Hear some sagas

Visitors to Jórvík wanting to read about the Vikings in Old Norse may be disappointed. Old Norse did not become a written language until the 13th century. This is when the sagas were written – long, epic poems about famous Vikings and their exploits. However, time travellers should not be too disappointed. The sagas were based on the long poems told by skalds at Viking feasts and you can attend such an event at the King's Hall (see pages 14–15).

Top Tip

Look out for some street names

Time travellers should look out for street names in Jórvík that sound the same in 21st century York. These include 'Myglagata', meaning the 'Great Street', which later became 'Micklegate'.

Speaking Old Norse

English-speaking visitors from the 21st century will find that many of their words originate from Old Norse. Learning some of these familiar-sounding words will help you communicate with your Viking hosts. They include:

- Knifr (knife)
- Sala (sale)
- Mugge (mug)
- Kaka (cake)
- Rotinn (rotten)
- Gefa (give)
- Gestr (guest)

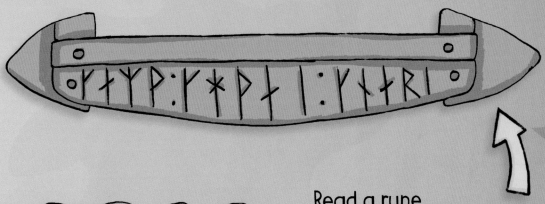

Read a rune

Eager time-travelling readers will be pleased to discover some written Viking words. Despite not presently having a written language, the Vikings do have runes. The runic alphabet consists of 16 letters that are carved on to wood, bone or stone. With the runes, the Vikings can construct very simple sentences, such as 'Thorfast made a good comb.' Larger runestones are commonly used to show landmarks, such as bridges and roads, or to mark the graves of the dead.

York Minster

MAKE TIME FOR THE HOLY MINSTER

No visit to Jórvík would be complete without stopping in at York Minster, the city church. The first wooden York Minster was built in the 7th century and was later replaced by a stone church. Not all of the residents of Jórvík worship here. This is because under the Vikings, people follow a mixture of pagan and Christian religions.

Odin

Sleipnir

Thor

Frejya

Pagan gods

Visitors to Jórvík will see evidence of the pagan Viking gods all around. Coins are imprinted with the god Thor's hammer, pendants show the goddess Frejya and carved stones depict king of the gods, Odin, and his eight-legged horse, Sleipnir. For centuries, the Vikings have worshipped many gods who they believe control all events on Earth. They can please and appease these gods by making offerings, including animal and human sacrifices.

Christian gods

Time travellers may hear stories from Anglo-Saxon residents of Jórvík about how many churches Viking warriors have destroyed. This is mostly true. However, many Vikings are now converting to Christianity. Some are also worshipping a mixture of gods as the two religions overlap. This can be seen in recently carved stones that have the shape of a Christian cross but show Viking warriors and creatures from pagan mythology. In time, however, all of the Vikings will convert and the homeland countries of Denmark, Sweden and Norway will become Christian.

Top Tip

Watch out for smoke

Despite some Jórvík Vikings accepting worshippers of the Christian faith, there are others who have trouble with the new religion. Long after the Vikings leave Jórvík a band of Danish raiders will burn York Minster to the ground in 1075. So, watch out for arson attacks while you are there!

◀ From the 11th century, people built another York Minster on the site of the Anglo-Saxon church. People continued to add to the Minister creating the magnificent cathedral you can visit today.

VISIT QUICK!

Under the Vikings, Jórvík is a prosperous, place that time travellers love to visit. The good times, however, will not last forever. Despite King Alfred the Great's peace deal of 878, many Anglo-Saxons don't want the Vikings in England. So visit quick while Jórvík is still in Viking hands!

The fall of Jórvík

Although Jórvík flourished under Viking rule it was never a stable place. From its conquest in CE 866, rulers came and went as Danish Vikings fought with Irish-based Vikings for control. In 927, the city was captured by the Anglo-Saxon King Athelstan only to be retaken by the Vikings 12 years later. In 944, the city was once again conquered by the Anglo-Saxons but retaken by Norwegian king Erik Bloodaxe in 948. Erik met his end after being ambushed in 954 and the English King Eadred took over. From that point it became an English city, and was later named York.

Erik Bloodaxe was king of Norway ▶ and Jorvik and the last Viking ruler of the Danelaw.

At the Battle of Stamford Bridge, Harald Hardrada led a Viking army of between 9,000 and 12,000 warriors against King Harold Godwinson of England. Harald lost.

The end of the Vikings

Although the Danelaw was taken back into English hands in 954, the Vikings still wanted England for themselves. In 1066, King Harald Hardrada of Norway landed in Northumbria with an army of 12,000 men and captured York. He then marched to meet English King Harold Godwinson at the Battle of Stamford Bridge. Here, Harold defeated the Viking army but soon had bigger problems. An invading force of Normans were launching an attack from France. Harold's men marched south to meet William the Conqueror's army at the Battle of Hastings. Harold lost, and the Normans invaded England. The Vikings would not attempt to invade again and retreated back to their Scandinavian homelands. Here, as the countries became Christian, the Vikings and their raiding ways ceased to exist.

William the Conqueror was related to Rollo – a Viking who had been awarded land in Normandy by French King Charles the Simple to stop him attacking Paris.

GLOSSARY

Amber A hard, yellow-brown substance that formed in ancient times. It is often used in jewellery.

Archaeologist A person who looks at ancient objects and buildings to learn about human history.

Brooch An ornament attached to a person's clothing with a large pin.

Conquer To take control of a place or people by force.

Hospitable Friendly and welcoming to guests.

Hygiene Keeping clean to stay healthy or prevent disease.

Legacy Something left behind or handed down from the past by an ancestor.

Longship A Viking sea-going ship that used both oars and sails for speed.

Monastery The buildings occupied by a community of monks.

Outlawed Made something illegal or unacceptable.

Rune A letter of the ancient Germanic alphabet.

Scabbard A sheath for keeping a sword.

Shire A county, particularly in England.

Skald An ancient Scandinavian word for a poet.

Thatch Straw, reeds and similar material used to cover a roof.

Treaty An agreement made between two groups of people, often to end a war.

Viking A Scandinavian warrior famous for attacking settlements in Europe between the 8th and 11th centuries.

FURTHER INFORMATION

Books

Everyday Life, Art and Culture (Discover the Vikings), John C. Miles, Franklin Watts 2016

Vikings (Britain in the Past), Moira Butterfield, Franklin Watts, 2017

Vikings (Explore!), Jane Bingham, Wayland, 2017

Vikings (What They Don't Tell You About), Robert Fowke, Wayland, 2013

The Vikings in Britain (Tracking Down), Moira Butterfield, Franklin Watts, 2013

Websites

An interactive BBC website for children all about the Vikings: **www.bbc.co.uk/education/topics/ztyr9j6**

A museum website belonging to the Jorvik Viking Centre, with information and images: **www.jorvikvikingcentre.co.uk**

A National Geographic website for children with easy to understand facts: **www.natgeokids.com/uk/discover/history/general-history/10-facts-about-the-vikings/**

A BBC website for primary school children about the Vikings and their everyday lives: **www.bbc.co.uk/schools/primaryhistory/vikings/**

A website designed to help primary school children with their homework: **primaryhomeworkhelp.co.uk/vikings.html**

INDEX

afterlife 20, 22–23
Anglo-Saxons 4, 6, 9, 12, 27
archaeologists 4–5

Battle of Hastings 29
Battle of Stamford Bridge 29
beliefs 20, 22–23, 26–27
blacksmiths 7, 20–21
burials 9, 20, 22–23

cemeteries 7, 22–23
Christianity 22, 26–27, 29
cleanliness 5, 10, 12
cloaks 18–19
clothing 18–19
coins 5, 26
cooking 13
Coppergate 16–17
craftspeople 8, 13, 16–17, 20–21

Danelaw 6, 9, 28–29
Denmark 6–7, 24, 27–28
duels 8, 21

East Anglia 9
Eboracum 6
entertainment 13–15
Eoforwic 6, 9

feasts 14–15, 22, 24
Fólkvangr 22
food 13–15
France 5, 8, 29
Freyja 22, 26

games 13
gods and goddesses 22, 26–27
graves 9, 22–23, 25
Great Invasion 9
Greenland 7, 11

Hnefatafl 13
homes/houses 6, 8, 12–13

Iceland 7, 17
Ireland 5, 7–8, 11, 17, 24–, 28
Ivar the Boneless 9

jewellery 16, 19
King Alfred the Great 9
King Athelstan 28
King Eadred 28
King Eric Bloodaxe 28
King Harald Hardrada 29
King Harold Godwinson 29
King William the Conqueror 29

King's Hall 7, 14–15, 24

languages 7, 11, 24–25
Lindisfarne 8
longhouses 12
longships 8, 10–11, 22

map 6–7
markets 5
merchants 8, 10–11, 17
Mercia 9
monasteries 7–8

Newfoundland 7
Normans 29
Northumbria, kingdom of 4, 9, 29
Norway 7, 24, 27–29

Odin 22, 26
Old Norse 11, 24–25

pagans 26–27
poems 15, 24
pottery/pots 17

quayside 7, 10–11

Ragnor Lodbrok 9
Ragnarók 22
raids, Viking 7–8, 11, 27, 29
religion 22–23, 26–27, 29

River Ouse 10
Romans 6, 14
runes 23, 25
runestones 23, 25
Russia 5, 7, 11

sagas 24
Scandinavia 4, 6–7, 17, 29
ships 8, 10–11
shops/shopkeepers 4, 6, 8, 16–17
silver 5, 8, 14, 16–17, 19
skalds 15, 20, 24
slaves 5
Sweden 7, 24, 27

tattoos 8, 18
Thor 26
toilets 12
trade 4–5, 7–8, 10–11, 16–17
Turkey 5, 11

Valhalla 22

warriors 4, 7–9, 14, 20, 22, 27, 29
weapons 20–21, 23
Wessex 9
workshops 16

York Minister 7, 26–27